DATE DUE

NOV 1 6 2000		
APR 2 3 2002		
		Printed in USA

HIGHSMITH #45230

America's Game

Detroit Tigers

Bob Italia

ABDO & Daughters
PUBLISHING

Published by Abdo & Daughters, 4940 Viking Dr., Suite 622, Edina, MN 55435.

Copyright ©1997 by Abdo Consulting Group, Inc., Pentagon Tower, P.O. Box 36036, Minneapolis, Minnesota 55435. International copyrights reserved in all countries. No part of this book may be reproduced in any form without written permission from the publisher. Printed in the United States.

Cover photo: Allsport
Interior photos: Wide World Photo, pages 1, 5, 9, 11, 13, 14, 16, 20, 21, 22, 23, 25, 27.

Edited by Paul Joseph

Library of Congress Cataloging–in–Publication Data

Italia, Bob, 1955-
  Detroit Tigers / Bob Italia
       p. cm. — (America's game)
  Includes index.
  Summary: Provides a detailed history of one of baseball's oldest teams, the Detroit Tigers.
  ISBN   1-56239-677-3
  1. Detroit Tigers (Baseball team)—Juvenile literature.
[1. Detroit Tigers (Baseball team)—History 2. Baseball—History.]
I. Title. II. Series.
GV875.D6I83   1997
796.357'64'0977434—dc20   96-23779
                                                CIP

Contents

Detroit Tigers

The Detroit Tigers are among baseball's oldest teams. Throughout the club's long history, Tiger fans have seen some of the worst, and best, baseball players and teams play before them.

Perhaps the most famous player was Hall-of-Famer Ty Cobb, a career .367 hitter who played in the early 1900s. After a long championship drought, slugger Hank Greenberg led the Tigers to the top of the division in the 1930s and 1940s—including two World Series championships.

The Tigers floundered for nearly two decades before another championship team emerged in the mid-1960s. This time, two dominant pitchers led the way: Mickey Lolich and Denny McLain. Lolich's tough performance in the 1968 World Series earned him Most Valuable Player (MVP) honors, while McLain racked up an amazing 31 victories during the regular season.

After that championship team eventually crumbled, Detroit ran away and hid from the rest of the league again. They did not field a successful team again until the mid 1980s. This remarkable squad,

Facing page: Cecil Fielder watches his 50th homer of 1990 fly into the left field stands during a game against the New York Yankees.

led by power pitcher Jack Morris and slugging catcher Lance Parrish, earned Detroit another World Championship in 1984, when they won a team-record 104 games. But like so many other Detroit teams before them, they quickly crumbled, leaving fans wondering when the Tigers would come roaring back.

Slugger Cecil Fielder became the star of the 1990s. But then he was traded. Ruben Sierra took his place in the lineup and performed well. But without a supporting cast, Detroit fans may have to wait a while longer before they see their beloved Tigers playing for another championship.

The Detroits

Professional baseball came to Detroit in 1881. Back then the "Detroits" belonged to the National League (NL) and played at Recreation Park. Detroit Mayor W. G. Thompson owned the team. They won the NL pennant in 1887.

Despite success on the field, the team had difficulty making money, and finally folded in 1888. In 1894, Major League Baseball returned to Detroit. The owner of the new franchise was Wayne County Sheriff James D. Burns.

The new team did not have a name at first. Sportswriters called it "Detroit," "the Detroits," or "the Wolverines," after the University of Michigan. The name "Tigers" came from *Detroit Free Press* box scores under the headline "Notes of the Detroit Tigers of 1895." By the following year, it was the accepted franchise name. Players began wearing tiger-striped stockings.

Detroit never finished higher than third place in the Western League. But enough fans supported the team to keep it going. Players often wore the same unwashed uniforms for weeks at a time. The team's new home, Bennett Park, was built on top of cobblestones. Hard-hit balls often took bad bounces. The ballpark was small. It seated only 6,000 customers and did not have a dressing room for the visiting team.

American League Tigers

In 1901, the Western League changed its name to the American League (AL) and gained acceptance nationwide. The Tigers' AL home debut was on April 25 at Bennett Park. Milwaukee led 13-4 when the Tigers came to bat for the last time in the game. Detroit scored 10 runs to win 14-13. The Tigers finished 74-61 under manager George Stallings. He left the organization that same year.

At the end of the 1901 season, Burns sold the Tigers to insurance man Samuel F. Angus. Angus appointed Frank J. Navin to manage the team's finances. In 1902, the Tigers plunged to seventh place. Angus soon put the team up for sale. Determined to keep the Tigers in Detroit, Navin searched for a new owner. He caught the attention of millionaire lumber baron William Clyman Yawkey, who agreed to buy the club. But Yawkey died before the deal was completed.

Refusing to give up, Navin turned to Yawkey's son, William Hoover Yawkey. The younger Yawkey bought the Tigers for $50,000 and gave Navin $5,000 worth of stock in the team. From there, Navin took over and helped build a successful franchise.

But the process took time. In 1903, two of the first star players—pitcher "Wild Bill" Donovan and outfielder "Wahoo Sam" Crawford—joined the team. The Tigers improved to fifth place in 1903, but then slipped back to seventh the following season.

At the start of the 1905 season, Bill Armour became the new manager. With Crawford, third baseman Bill Coughlin, and outfielder Matty McIntyre on the roster, Armour had much work to do. Then a young rookie arrived in Detroit in August 1905.

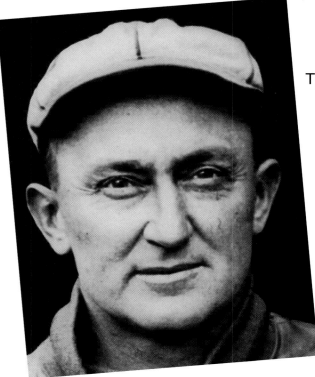

Tyrus R. Cobb.

Ty Cobb

Rookie Tyrus Raymond "Ty" Cobb was 18 years old and weighed just 160 pounds. He had just finished a season with the Augusta, Georgia, team in the South Atlantic League. On August 30, 1905, Cobb signed a contract to play baseball for $1,800 a year.

Some experts say Cobb was the greatest player of all time. For 23-straight years, he hit better than .300, won 12 batting championships, and at one time held 90 major-league records, including the highest career batting average (.367)—a mark that still stands today.

Cobb was not an imposing figure. But he played with an intensity that intimidated other players. He would stop at nothing to win—like sinking his spikes into opponents who tried to tag him out as he slid into a base.

 9

Cobb's teammates did not know how to respond to him. Manager Armour tried to instruct Cobb, with little success. Cobb spent much time on the bench during 1906, and the Tigers finished in sixth place. Navin fired Armour at the end of the 1906 season and hired Hugh A. Jennings. Jennings was Detroit's first player-manager and showed much enthusiasm. He saw that Cobb was an outstanding player. He made allowances for Cobb's moods and let him play his own style.

The special treatment worked wonders. In 1907, Cobb won the first of his 12 batting titles, hitting .350 for the season. Cobb and 3 pitchers—who each won more than 20 games—earned Detroit its first American League Championship.

In the 1907 World Series, the Tigers played the Chicago Cubs. The Series opened at Chicago with a rare 3-3 tie game, which was called because of darkness. Chicago then beat Detroit in four-straight games to claim the championship.

Discouraged by the Tigers' loss, Yawkey sold Navin enough stock to make Navin half owner of the club by 1908. Navin soon became president.

The Tigers finished in first place with a 90-63 record. The title was not decided until the final game of the season, when Detroit finished one-half game ahead of the Cleveland Naps. In the World Series, the Tigers again met the Cubs. Unfortunately, the Cubs won in five games.

Detroit finished on top of the American League again in 1909 with a 98-54 record. In the World Series, the Tigers met the Pittsburgh Pirates and their star, Honus Wagner. This time, the Tigers were favored to win the Series. But Pittsburgh proved just as tough as Chicago, winning the World Championship in seven games—the last by a shutout. The Tigers would not appear in the World Series again for a quarter of a century.

Mediocrity

In the following decade, the Tigers fell in the standings. The only exception was the 1915 season, when Detroit won 100 games for the first time in their history. But they still failed to win the pennant when Boston won 101 games.

During the World War I years, the Tigers slipped back into mediocrity. In 1918 and 1920, they finished seventh. In 1919, Cobb's .384 average was good enough for his 12th batting title.

The early 1920s were a rebuilding time for Detroit. Slowly the core of another championship team was assembled. In 1924, second baseman Charley Gehringer joined the team. Power hitter Hank Greenberg was added in 1930. Pitcher "Schoolboy" Rowe signed on in 1933, and hitting star Leon "The Goose" Goslin came in a trade with Washington in 1934. They eventually propelled the Tigers back into post-season play.

Tigers' pitcher Lynwood "Schoolboy" Rowe warms up before a game in 1935.

Moving Into Contention

In 1934, the Tigers moved into contention for the league championship. Navin bought Mickey Cochrane's services from the Philadelphia Athletics and made him a player-manager. With Schoolboy Rowe's 24-8 record leading the way, the 1934 Tigers won the pennant by a seven-game margin over the New York Yankees and returned the World Series to Detroit.

The 1934 World Series was a seven-game war against the St. Louis Cardinals, which the Tigers lost. The team had a hard time recovering the following season. They were in last place during April and in sixth on May 28.

But then the Tigers rallied. By the end of July, Detroit held first place. They won the pennant by a three-game margin. Greenberg batted .328 with 36 home runs (HRs), 13 triples, 46 doubles, and 170 runs batted in (RBIs). He was named the American League's MVP.

Champion Tigers

The 1935 World Series was a rematch against the Chicago Cubs. The Tigers were favored to win their first championship. But in the second game, Greenberg suffered a broken wrist that eliminated him from the Series. Cochrane was forced to shuffle his lineup.

Just when it looked bad for Detroit, the Tigers rallied to take the Series with strong offensive performances by Gehringer and Pete Fox. On October 7, 1935, Detroit won its first World Championship. The fans celebrated all night, then held a ticker-tape parade in honor of their heroes.

Hank Greenberg tries to slide home during the 1935 World Series, but is tagged out by Cubs' catcher Gabby Hartnett.

No one was happier than Navin. But within a month of the World Series victory, Navin suffered a heart attack and died. Briggs quickly bought Navin's share of the Tigers and became sole owner of the franchise. His first years as owner-president were difficult. In 1936, Cochrane suffered a nervous breakdown. Managing duties were turned over to coach Del Baker. Detroit finished in second place.

Cochrane returned to his job in 1937, but nearly lost his life when he was struck on the left temple by a pitch. He spent four days in critical condition. After his recovery, he tried to return as manager, but he had little success. Briggs fired him early in the 1938 season.

The Tigers finished $26^1/_2$ games out of first place in 1939. But then, in 1940, General Manager Jack Zeller added pitcher Louis Norman "Bobo" Newsom.

During the 1940 season, Newsom won 21 games for Detroit. The Tigers fought hard all season long and had a chance to win the pennant in a three-game series against second-place Cleveland during the last weekend of the season. The Tigers needed to win only one of the three games to clinch the pennant, so rookie pitcher Floyd Giebell got the start against Cleveland's ace, Bob Feller.

Surprisingly, Giebell shut the Indians out, and the Tigers claimed first place. In the 1940 World Series, they met the Cincinnati Reds. The Series stretched to seven games, with Newsom winning two for Detroit. Newsom got the start in the seventh game, but lost 2-1.

Tigers' pitcher Louis "Bobo" Newsom shows off his pitching style before the 1940 World Series against the Cincinnati Reds.

The War Years

On May 17, 1941, Hank Greenberg became the first American Leaguer to be drafted into the U.S. Army. Greenberg's departure left the Tigers in fourth place.

All of baseball suffered from World War II as more and more players left their teams to fight overseas. The game was played by a ragtag collection of players. Besides Greenberg, Detroit lost Gehringer, Barney McCoskey, Pat Mullin, Birdie Tebbetts, Al Benton, Freddie Hutchinson, and Dick Wakefield.

By 1945, some players returned to their teams—including Greenberg. He smacked a line-drive home run that clinched the 1945 pennant for the Tigers on the last day of the season.

The Tigers played the Cubs in the 1945 World Series. Each team used 19 players, trying to find a winning combination. The Series stretched to seven games. In Game 7, the Tigers scored five runs in the first inning and coasted to a 9-3 win over the Cubs for their second World Series title.

Tigers' slugger and 1949 batting champion George Kell
receives a silver bat from American League President Will
Harridge.

Batting Champions

Though the late 1940s and 1950s did not bring any world championships to Detroit, it was still an exciting time for Tiger fans. Third baseman George Kell won the 1949 batting championship on his very last at-bat of the season. In 1955, Al Kaline became the youngest hitter ever to win a batting championship. And in 1959, Harvey Kuenn hit .353.

The 1950s also brought a change in Tiger ownership. Briggs sold the team in 1956 to an 11-man syndicate, one of whom was John E. Fetzer—the next great leader of the Detroit organization. Fetzer gained control of the Tigers in 1960.

The Tigers had problems with managers in the 1960s. In 1965, Charley Dressen suffered a heart attack during spring training. He was temporarily replaced by coach Bob Swift. The following year, Dressen suffered another heart attack. Swift took over again but soon developed lung cancer. Frank Skaff relieved him midway through the 1966 season. By year's end, both Dressen and Swift had died.

In 1967, the Tigers hired Mayo Smith as manager. The team started showing promise. Al Kaline was still hitting the ball. Norm Cash was a consistent .300 hitter. And the pitching staff had Mickey Lolich and Denny McLain.

The 1967 pennant race was one of the tightest ever, as the Tigers battled the Boston Red Sox and the Minnesota Twins for first place. The Red Sox won the pennant on the final day of the season when Detroit lost at home.

Detroit

Ty Cobb hit better than
.300 for 23 straight years,
winning 12 batting
championships.

In 1934, pitcher Schoolboy
Rowe led the pennant-
winning Tigers with a 24-8
record.

In 1934, Hank Greenberg was named
the American League's MVP.

Bobo Newsom won
21 games for
Detroit in 1940.

In 1968, pitcher Denny McLain won an incredible 31 regular season games.

Mark "The Bird" Fidrych was named Rookie of the Year in 1976.

In 1993, manager Sparky Anderson won his 2,000th game as a professional baseball manager.

Slugger Cecil Fielder led the American League in RBIs three years in a row—1990, 1991, and 1992—the first player since Babe Ruth to do so.

Denny McLain pitching towards his 30th win September 14, 1968.

The Best Season Ever

In 1968, the Tigers had one of their best seasons ever. They seized first place on May 10, and never gave it up, finishing the season with 103 wins.

Denny McLain emerged as the team leader. He won an incredible 31 regular season games—the first pitcher to do so since 1934. The Tigers then prepared to meet the St. Louis Cardinals in the World Series.

In Game 1, McLain lasted six innings as Cardinal pitcher Bob Gibson shut out the Tigers 4-0. Detroit evened the Series in Game 2 with an easy 8-1 victory behind Mickey Lolich. Then the Cardinals won back-to-back games and took a 3-1 Series lead.

The Tigers refused to give up. Lolich returned to the mound for Game 5 and led the Tigers to a 5-3 win. McLain rebounded in Game 6 as the Tigers pounded out a 13-1 victory. With the Series tied 3-3, Detroit had to face Bob Gibson in the final game. Lolich came back with only two days' rest to face the Cardinal ace. Gibson held the Tigers scoreless through six innings, but Detroit finally rallied and won the game 4-1. The Tigers were World Champions once again.

Down Time

The Tigers were unable to stay on top of the baseball world. In 1969, they finished second in the new Eastern Division of the American League. At the end of the following year, McLain was traded to the Senators. The championship team was falling apart.

In 1971, the Tigers hired Billy Martin as manager. Martin performed well, and in 1972 Detroit won the AL East. But the American League Championship Series (ALCS) went to the Oakland Athletics in five games. After that season, Detroit crumbled. Martin left midway through the 1973 season. Ralph Houk replaced him. For the rest of the decade, the Tigers finished no better than third, and they finished last two of those years. They even lost a record 19 games in a row in 1975.

Billy Martin before Game 1 of the 1972 ALCS against the Oakland Athletics.

Tigers' rookie pitcher Mark "The Bird" Fidrych talks to the baseball before a 1976 game against the Baltimore Orioles.

The Bird And Other Stars

Despite the team's poor performance, the Tigers remained entertaining. In 1976, pitcher Mark "The Bird" Fidrych joined the team. Fidrych was a peculiar but talented pitcher. He talked to the ball between pitches, stomped the mound, and even patted the dirt. The fans packed the stadium whenever he pitched.

After compiling a 19-9 record with a league-leading 2.34 earned run average (ERA), Fidrych was named Rookie of the Year in 1976. But in 1977, he injured his knee during spring training and never pitched effectively in the majors again. His entire career in Detroit lasted only 48 games.

In 1977, the Tigers started turning things around. Another star pitcher arrived. His name was Jack Morris. Shortstop Alan Trammell, infielder Lou Whitaker, and catcher Lance Parrish joined the club in 1978. Manager Sparky Anderson came to Detroit in 1979. Slugger Kirk Gibson and pitcher Dan Petry were added in 1980.

Suddenly, the Tigers had a talented lineup and strong leadership. Fans expected greatness out of this new Tiger squad.

The Tigers finished the strike-shortened 1981 season in second place. Though disappointed with the outcome, the Tigers were ready to challenge for the division championship the following year. But injuries to key players prevented any improvement.

In 1983, Detroit got a new owner—Thomas S. Monaghan, founder of the Domino's Pizza chain. Morris recorded his first 20-win season. Parrish blasted 27 home runs and knocked in 114 runs. Parrish, Whitaker, and Trammell won Gold Glove Awards. But the Tigers finished the year in second place with a 92-70 record. Fans wondered when this talented team would finally break out on top.

Tigers' manager Sparky Anderson contemplates his next move during a game against the Milwaukee Brewers.

A Team Of Destiny

They didn't have to wait long to find out. In 1984, the Tigers jumped out to an amazing 35-5 start and never looked back. They won 104 games and easily captured first place in the division.

But they did not stop there. This was a team of destiny, and it took only five games for the Tigers to defeat the San Diego Padres for the World Series crown. With the victory, Anderson became the first major league manager to win championships in both leagues.

Anderson kept the Tigers competitive through most of the 1980s, but it was not easy. Gibson and Morris suffered injuries in 1985. Parrish suffered a season-ending back injury in 1986. Still, the team received strong pitching from reliever Willie Hernandez, Petry, and Frank Tanana. The Tigers finished in third place in 1985 and 1986.

In 1987, the Tigers battled the Toronto Blue Jays for first place. The lead in the American League East changed four times over the final 50 games of the season. Finally, to determine the division title, Detroit and Toronto went head-to-head in 7 of the last 11 games.

All seven Detroit-Toronto games were decided by one run. The Blue Jays took three of the first four in Toronto. But the Tigers rallied to win the fourth game in 13 innings.

Trailing Toronto by one game, the Tigers faced the Blue Jays in Detroit for a final three-game series. In front of sellout crowds, the Tigers won all three games. The clincher came on a Sunday afternoon, when Tanana shut out the Jays 1-0. Larry Herndon's solo home run was the difference.

Jack Morris and Kirk Gibson celebrate after winning the 1984
World Series against the San Diego Padres.

Detroit had won six of the last eight games of the season to clinch
the title. It seemed destiny was on their side again. But the Minnesota
Twins ended the Tigers' fairy tale season in the best-of-seven ALCS.

Despite the playoff setback, the Tigers had become the most
successful team in the American League during the 1980s. Detroit
had finished in third place or better every year between 1983 and
1988. And they had won the American League East twice.

But suddenly, everything began to collapse. Star players left the
team for more money. By 1989, Morris, Gibson, Parrish, and Petry
were gone. In just one season, the Tigers plunged from second place
to last with a 59-103 record.

Cecil Arrives

The Tigers rebounded in the 1990s. Slugger Cecil Fielder joined the team in 1990. His home run hitting helped Detroit to a third-place finish in 1990. They tied for second place in 1991. Fielder also led the league in RBIs three years in a row—1990, 1991, and 1992—the first player since Babe Ruth to do so. Unfortunately, the Tigers slipped back under .500 in 1992, with a 75-87 record and a sixth-place finish. That same year, Monaghan sold the baseball club to Michael Ilitch, who owned the Little Caesar's pizza chain.

Sparky Anderson won his 2,000th game as a professional baseball manager on April 15, 1993, when the Tigers beat the Oakland A's 3-2. The team played well all season long, but fell short in their bid to capture a pennant, as their 85-77 record left them 10 games behind Toronto and tied for third place with the Baltimore Orioles.

Fielder and Mickey Tettleton led the way offensively. Fielder smacked 30 home runs and drove in 117 runs, while Tettleton launched 32 homers and had 110 RBIs. Travis Fryman had a fine season as well, with 22 homers and 97 RBIs. And Alan Trammell led the team in hitting, with a sizzling .329 batting average. Relief pitcher Mike Henneman finished the season with 24 saves, while John Doherty led the starting pitchers with a 14-11 record.

Detroit could not get it going in 1994, but neither could the rest of the league. A players' strike halted the season and left Detroit in last place with a 53-62 record.

The 1995 season proved almost as bad. The Tigers' 60-84 mark left them in fourth place, 26 games behind first-place Boston. The few bright spots were Lou Whitaker, who led the team with a .293

batting average, and surprising Chad Curtis, who socked 21 home runs. Although Fielder hit a team-high 31 homers, he only drove in 82 runs and struck out 116 times. Pitcher Mike Henneman had a sparkling 1.53 ERA and a team-high 18 saves. Starter David Wells posted a 10-3 record despite little offensive support.

Cecil Fielder watches the flight of the ball at the home run contest during All-Star festivities on July 12, 1993.

Roaring Tigers

With the departure of Sparky Anderson, Lou Whitaker, and Kirk Gibson before the start of the 1996 season, the Tigers lost a combined 46 years of team service. Shortstop Alan Trammell returned for his 19th season, but slugger Cecil Fielder was traded to the Yankees in midseason for Ruben Sierra. The Tigers clearly had embarked on a new era. It would not begin with a championship.

Rookie manager Buddy Bell was charged with the difficult task of getting the team moving in the right direction. Mark Lewis and Chris Gomez were the young infielders designated to replace the record-setting combination of Whitaker and Trammell, separated after 1,918 appearances together. If Bell can one day piece together a solid starting rotation, the Tigers could roar again.

Glossary

All-Star: A player who is voted by fans as the best player at one position in a given year.

American League (AL): An association of baseball teams formed in 1900 which make up one-half of the major leagues.

American League Championship Series (ALCS): A best-of-seven-game playoff with the winner going to the World Series to face the National League Champions.

Batting Average: A baseball statistic calculated by dividing a batter's hits by the number of times at bat.

Earned Run Average (ERA): A baseball statistic which calculates the average number of runs a pitcher gives up per nine innings of work.

Fielding Average: A baseball statistic which calculates a fielder's success rate based on the number of chances the player has to record an out.

Hall of Fame: A memorial for the greatest baseball players of all time located in Cooperstown, New York.

Home Run (HR): A play in baseball where a batter hits the ball over the outfield fence scoring everyone on base as well as the batter.

Major Leagues: The highest ranking associations of professional baseball teams in the world, currently consisting of the American and National Baseball Leagues.

Minor Leagues: A system of professional baseball leagues at levels below Major League Baseball.

National League (NL): An association of baseball teams formed in 1876 which make up one-half of the major leagues.

National League Championship Series (NLCS): A best-of-seven-game playoff with the winner going to the World Series to face the American League Champions.

Pennant: A flag which symbolizes the championship of a professional baseball league.

Pitcher: The player on a baseball team who throws the ball for the batter to hit. The pitcher stands on a mound and pitches the ball toward the strike zone area above the plate.

Plate: The place on a baseball field where a player stands to bat. It is used to determine the width of the strike zone. Forming the point of the diamond-shaped field, it is the final goal a base runner must reach to score a run.

RBI: A baseball statistic standing for *runs batted in.* Players receive an RBI for each run that scores on their hits.

Rookie: A first-year player, especially in a professional sport.

Slugging Percentage: A statistic which points out a player's ability to hit for extra bases by taking the number of total bases hit and dividing it by the number of at bats.

Stolen Base: A play in baseball when a base runner advances to the next base while the pitcher is delivering his pitch.

Strikeout: A play in baseball when a batter is called out for failing to put the ball in play after the pitcher has delivered three strikes.

Triple Crown: A rare accomplishment when a single player finishes a season leading their league in batting average, home runs, and RBIs. A pitcher can win a Triple Crown by leading the league in wins, ERA, and strikeouts.

Walk: A play in baseball when a batter receives four pitches out of the strike zone and is allowed to go to first base.

World Series: The championship of Major League Baseball played since 1903 between the pennant winners from the American and National Leagues.

Index